GOLDEN RAIN
THE UNTOLD REVENGE

BY SONIA ASHNA

Dorrance Publishing Co
585 Alpha Drive
Suite 103
Pittsburgh, PA 15238
Visit our website at *www.dorrancebookstore.com*

ISBN: 979-8-89341-485-1
eISBN: 979-8-89341-984-9

ACKNOWLEDGEMENT

I give my thanks and gratitude to my parents, Tom and Shakeela.

My three siblings, Waz, Irph, and Ann, and my other family members and friends who supported me.

My dear friends, Letesha and Bibi.

Special thanks to Dr. Rosh Khan, President - of ACE Consulting Group.

Thanks you to you, my Cocomoco, for being an inspiration.

Thank you to Benjamin Altomari and Rachael Bindas at Dorrance Publishing Company.

My biggest and greatest thanks goes to God for always guiding me through and making ways.

INTRODUCTION

"As long as you live, you surely have to go through misfortune to overcome. But the final results depend on how you deal with it during and after the misfortunes." –Sonia

A touching and true story about someone who endured and overcame many types of adversities from a young age. The bitter days she endured made her stronger and bold. Most of the time, she felt lonely and devastated in her relationship. Until one day she had actual love. She had an experience of what real love is. She was waiting for a happy ending, but life had bigger surprises for her. But did she lose or did she gain in love?

GOLDEN RAIN
THE UNTOLD REVENGE

CHAPTER ONE

"Some things are better left unexpressed," she thought to herself as tears gently fell on her soft pink cheeks. "If only he knew." She quietly cried to herself, looking back at the picture that she kept on her phone.

Roman and Rosia were in a long-term relationship. But that came with complications, stumbling blocks, and many sacrifices, like every normal relationship. But this was just too complicated. They were close, yet far, the distance never reduced, physically, emotionally, and mentally. Roman lived in the USA, and Rosia lived in Guyana. Being in a long-distance relationship would make them love each other a little more, and wouldn't do any harm, they thought to themselves. But it wasn't until her fantasy became reality.

However, not all stories have a perfect ending. But will this one end happily? Every ending is a new beginning.

Most of the time she felt lonely and devastated in their relationship since Roman never prioritized her. Her prayer kept them together regardless of his actions towards her. She was a strong believer in prayers since that was all that she could have done.

Rosia and Roman met on a cloudy afternoon at a bus park after school and there they got into an argument. It started when she refused to be seated next to the driver, who happened to be Roman's father, Mr. Ray, who normally picked her up from school every afternoon, so that wasn't the first time Roman had seen her.

One day, Mr. Ray showed up late and she was there waiting on him after dance practice. Her long golden hair glittered in the sunlight, with a red rose on one side, matching her long lilac and white dress. He couldn't help but notice the princess-like damsel from just a few steps away.

And that was the first time he saw her. But she didn't notice him even though they were on the same bus. From then on, whenever he passed by her small town, he kept hoping that he would see her, even if it were just a small glimpse. However, he didn't, until two years after.

Two days after the incident, they met in a boat which they used as their means of transportation to and from school.

On their second encounter, she knew to herself that there was something peculiar about him. That was the last day they had seen each other for that year 2007. The following year brought her disappointments and irreplaceable happiness. That year changed her life forever.

The following year, 2008, she started to believe in love, something she never used to believe in, and it happened when she developed a crush on Keegan.

She was apprehensive about the new school year, however. She was preparing for her final exams so she focused less on Keegan. On the other hand, she and Roman kept bumping into each other often. One day he asked her if she was seeing anyone, and her response was, "Yes, I'm seeing many at the moment." But looking at his gloomy face, with assurance, she confessed that it was a joke. From that day on, he talked to her with self-confidence.

The rain kept pouring heavily like beads falling from above. The morning was dark and cold. Rosia and Roman ran into each other, where they had to share one umbrella. This brought them physically close. Both of them enjoyed the moment even though they got drenched in the muzzily cold rain. While all this excitement was happening, she was unaware that Keegan had seen it all the while.

Most afternoons after school, Roman and Rosia would sit together. She tried to figure out why it was that even though she thought she didn't like him, she still tolerated him. Most of the time, she seemed irritable whenever he went by because they kept arguing. However, the hatred disappeared and he would walk her to school frequently, but that didn't change the aggression between the two of them.

A few days before her final exams, she thought about whether or not she should tell Keegan how she felt. But as usual, Roman inadvertently came in the way. However, they both enjoyed upsetting each other because they didn't get along. But she didn't know that the same person she fought with, she would fight for. Like Louie used to tell her, "After hate is love."

Just before exams, she confided in her friends and sister about Keegan. She fell for his handsomeness and reserved personality. He was every girl's dream guy: tall and handsome. His looks matched his personality and she thought that they looked good together.

"Do you think I should let him know how I feel?" she whispered to Alice. But she supported her saying, "It's up to you if you want to."

Keegan and Alice were closer, while Theo and Jayda were close. Two sisters being friends with two brothers caused Rosia to think that was a bonus since Alice was dating Theo.

Words got back to Keegan and he was waiting for her to confess. He wanted to hear from her since it's better to hear from the horse's mouth. She dialed his number in anticipation of a blissful answer, but that was when she got her first heartbreak. If only she had confessed a few days ago before she had seen someone else, he would have accepted her.

While waiting on her friends three days later, she thought that they had already left, and the boat was about to close. With that, it was an unexpected arrival of Roman. He made her afternoon pretty much entertaining. While the two of them were having fun and the conversation was interesting, she didn't care to pay attention to who was looking. She was just being herself and they seemed joyful.

"Roman, there's something I want you to know, but I don't know how to explain."

To his dismay, he questioned himself. What could she possibly want to tell him?

"What is it you want to tell me now?" asked Roman, and these were her exact words: "Roman, I kind of like you, I'm interested in you."

"I want to know if you feel the same about me, and I want to know before I go home."

He just stood there blushing with excitement, asking in a low-toned voice, "What is your name?"

She was actually surprised that he didn't know her name. She then replied, "My name is Rosia, but most people call me Rosy."

"Okay, Rosy, don't fool me." But she explained to him how serious she was. His reply was touching. "Rosy, I love you, and I am serious."

After hearing his reply, her face lit up with a smile, asking, "So how was my drama? Do you think I can become an actress?"

With disappointment, he said, "Rosy, you are not serious about that. Is that just a game to you?"

Being the best drama student in her high school, she was known to be an outstanding actor.

When the boat reached across the other side of the river she then remembered that Keegan had wanted to talk to her, but he didn't have the chance since she was very much busy with Roman. Keegan later explained to their friends what he had seen between Roman and Rosia. Just when he was about to tell her that he liked her too. She realized that he saw everything that went on that day. That didn't bother her because she then realized that it was just a crush that didn't develop into love.

CHAPTER TWO

Trying to get home early that afternoon, she ran into Roman unexpectedly and they struck up a conversation as usual. But this time it was different, since she took his phone number, without giving hers to him. The friendship started on that day.

The next morning, she was waiting alone, waiting on her friends when Roman showed up; they argued about how inappropriate her clothes were. He then assisted her by fixing her baby doll top by making a bow at the back. Rosia's dream career was to be a fashion designer, a model, or any thing to do with entertainment, so she always seemed classy and in fashion.

In the boat that morning, they sat together, and she took one of his fallen eyelashes and asked him to make a wish.

"If I wish to have you, will it come true?" he asked.

"I don't know, Roman, but don't tell anyone what you wish for," she said softly to him. But did he really wish to have her?

That was the last day he walked her to school since she had to write her final exam. When they had almost reached he asked her for one side of her earring which she had made. As he collected the earrings, he said with confidence, "One day, these earrings will come together and make a pair again."

Without saying a word to him, she smiled, saying to herself, "What the hell is he talking about?"

He stood there watching her enter her school compound, forgetting that he was late for school.

He would call her every morning before he reached school since he couldn't see her, because she had finished school. One midday, she called him and to her surprise, a woman with a heavy voice answered rudely. But bravely, she talked to the woman who happened to be his mother.

It wasn't long after that day, summer, she decided to tell him how she felt about him, not even sure what she felt. After expressing her feelings, he thought that that was another prank of hers again. But was it? Or was she serious this time?

She tried to explain to him, but he said he had to think about it since he was afraid of her drama.

"Will he reciprocate?"

"I can't blame him if he rejects me." That was the thought that crossed her mind.

It was two days after that she had her answer. As forecasted, he felt the same way. She then knew that there was a difference between having a crush on someone and falling in love. Their relationship ignited, but did it last? Was it real?

She wanted to be with him every day, so she enrolled in a school not far from his school. Seeing them together, everyone started to make atrocious comments about the new and popular couple. Few of his friends even crossed the line and commented that he wasn't good enough for her, since she was beautiful while he was average-looking. But for her, he was handsome and she fell in love with him. Even though many guys were after her, she cared less and focused on her love.

Every morning she would wait for him, but he wasn't loyal to her. He never waited on her, not even one day. He cared less about her and cared more about his image in society. Despite the fact that he treated her like an option, she still loved him.

They would fight like they hated each other, but by the end of the day, they made up. And that was how their relationship was throughout the years.

CHAPTER THREE

Rosia and Roman's first day of the new year was a memorable one. While most couples celebrated New Year together, theirs were different. As the clock struck midnight in 2009, they had their first fight for the year and that too was over the phone, just after saying, "Happy New Year" and "I love you" to each other. It happened because of his carelessness and her obedience. He insisted that she go get herself soaked in the rain since she was fond of the rain. So that was exactly what she did, and that started the fight. That incident brought them almost close to a breakup. But as she would always say, "Let's mend it, instead of end it." That saved their relationship because she let go of her ego because she understood their relationship, as well as her boyfriend.

She wasn't mistreated by him alone, but by his family as well. They often tell her words as sharp as a knife. Being verbally abused by his mother, she knew to herself that she'd have to put up with a major fight by hiding all emotions. She did nothing about it.

Most times, they were seen arguing in public. It came to a point where Keegan commented, saying, "Do you see what you caused upon yourself?"

Feeling humiliated, she said nothing but smiled and walked away with tears in her eyes.

The dramas made her into a different person. She lost her self-esteem as well as herself. Her friends felt sorry for her and encouraged her to stop seeing Roman, but she was stubborn.

It was approaching his twenty-second birthday and she wanted to give him a present. Not having that kind of money to buy him something expensive, she sold some of her clothes and accessories. She put aside her pride and did what she had to. She never knew she had it in her until then.

"Rosy, you have to stop seeing that guy; he's trouble!" her mother yelled angrily.

Her parents disapproved of their daughter seeing him, but they were never as bad to him as his family was to her. They were well-spoken, and thus he thought that her parents supported their relationship.

CHAPTER FOUR

What were two people to do when they were in love and alone? It was early March and tempestuous rain raged with passion. That midday he left classes since he had planned on seeing her that afternoon. He got wet in the rain, and so did she.

While drying herself he gently wrapped his huge hands around her slim body. He slowly removed her short black dress. Upon doing so, he quietly asked, "Is it okay with you?"

She calmly replied, "Yes, but please be gentle; it's my first time."

"This is my first time too, my love, and I'm glad it's with you," he said.

He brushed his plump lips lightly across hers as she tightly caressed him. Their bodies merged together like a tree bringing water through its roots. And they made love for the first time. The afternoon was cloudy, and he did not want her to go home, since he immersed himself in her presence.

She, on the other hand, wanted to go home since it was getting dark and her family was expecting her to be there before night. She couldn't stop thinking about what happened earlier, but Roman, who was caring at the moment, gave her reasons not to worry. She was pleased that she lost her virginity to Roman and at the age of nineteen and not younger.

Her class finished before his since she was in a private computer class. But regardless, she waited on him the afternoon after classes.

Everything was going well until her parents restricted her from seeing him. She had to do home studies, and to add salt to wound, she was grounded. Being a stubborn girl, she figured out a way to continue her studies and keep in touch with him. But it wasn't for long.

"Rosia, I'm warning you for the last time, you have to stop seeing that guy," her mother shouted angrily.

"But what's wrong with seeing him, Mommy?"

"He will distract you from your studies."

"No, he won't, besides, he's a nice person, you will like him."

"Nice he probably is, but nice for you, and don't argue with me," she said angrily.

That disastrous event caused her to fear Friday the 13th.

Not long before he wrote his final exams, they had to separate because of her family. But she kept persevering.

"God, if he is the one for me, then let me see him; fix it all," she cried out silently.

Without any doubt, she went about her daily routine. It was hard not to see each other and in just a few days, he grew to resent her. It was hard enough for her to have problems with her family, but he was losing interest in her. That was heart-wrenching, but on the other hand, it was somehow inspiring, because she never knew how strong she was until she had no other choice but to be strong.

Alice, however, started to help her sister sneak out of the house to see Roman, and it worked out well. Many times, she lied to her parents to go see him. That went on until she made her teacher call and encouraged her parents to send her back to school.

But fate kept putting stones in her way. After gaining back some of her parent's trust, her mother made a deal with her that she could go back to school, but she had to pay her school fee. She didn't have a job, and with that, she had no income. Alice, however, convinced her mother to pay for tuition for one month.

It wasn't long after they received a call that a close relative from abroad was visiting, and that made her prayer come through. But for a different reason. She received some money and could hardly wait to deliver the marvelous news, so she called him immediately. But he also had news for her. As usual, she would listen to what he had to say first.

"Rosy, my driver's license expired, plus I have to fix other things and I don't have the money to do it," said Roman in a sad voice.

On hearing this, she knew it was either him or her. Living in a single-parent family at the moment was very tough. She knew for a fact that things wouldn't work out between them if she didn't go back to school. That was one of her biggest fears. Not wanting to tell him what she had to say, she told him that she would give him the money. He had no clue that she made such a sacrifice for him.

Not giving up on her prayers, she started to fast; being a Christian has taught her to have strong faith in God. And God kept showing her how great He was. The next morning, Alice convinced their mother to pay for her studies until she got a job. But that also came with the price of a strict curfew.

The first few weeks, she made sure she was home early and everyone was pleased. While in school, she kept sending out job applications to almost every business place she knew. She had little time on hand, but no one hired her since there were no vacancies.

Life just kept hitting her with a heavy bat. She and Isabel, Roman's mother, were out together. Like two mature people, they were getting along until the conversation started to get challenging. It was then Isabel pointed out that if Rosia wanted her son, she should get a job.

Waking up very early the next morning with a positive thought, she was ready to face the day. After discussing the job that she was going to, Roman didn't seem to be considerate.

It was very tremendously difficult dealing with family issues, financial issues, and on the other hand, an irresponsible boyfriend at the same time, because of whom she had to face all this. But she had to endure it all by herself.

She knew that she was well qualified for the job she was seeking. Without an application, she went bravely. Her first hurdle was the security guard, and he let her in since it was raining heavily. Being the first applicant, she sat there all by herself, waiting to be called in to take a test. After taking the test, she assured herself that she would get the job.

The first thing she did was to call Roman, but he wasn't delighted. While explaining the procedure to him and that she had to wait to be called, he angrily said to her that she would never get the job. He kept saying that she was wasting her time. She confidently stood there, listening to him discouraging her.

Swiftly came the month of June, which made a year for their strained relationship. They didn't plan how to spend it.

She asked to spend the day with him since they had partially spent time together during the past few months.

It was August and yet there was no reply from the company. She was disheartened but she still waited patiently with hope. Sitting in her parents' flower garden with Alice and their friends was a normal habit. But that afternoon was an unpredictable one. The phone rang and her mother answered. It was a stranger on the other line who wanted to talk to her.

Before telling anyone what the call was about, she quickly dialed Roman's number. After conveying the news to him, she let the others know that she procured ninety-five percent marks for them.

CHAPTER FIVE

Now that he finished his schooling and she started her first job as a quality control agent for a telecommunication company, they seldom saw each other. It was quite challenging sometimes, but there wasn't anything that she couldn't fix. She always found a way to make things happen.

It was not fully three months before she started to sacrifice her job to spend time with him. She started to absent herself from work and sometimes got to work late, but it wasn't worth it at all.

Her trembling hands picked up the phone, as darkness clouded her mind. Her head became numb when she began to read the text messages she had seen written on his phone. He had been cheating on her for the past months. She then knew the reasons for his negligence. But she blamed herself, for she made many sacrifices even though he showed her who he was. Being blinded by what she called love, it wasn't long after he convinced her to give him another chance.

Staying in a relationship with a self-centered, insensitive, and shallow man was the worst thing she did to herself.

Her best friend, Britney, was always there for her. She knew when she was not happy. Even though they didn't hang out often, they communicated well on the phone. Many times, she would try to hide her sad emotions, but at some point, it all fell apart.

Knowing that she didn't deserve such treatment, she kept remembering Keegan's words. She didn't complain because it was indeed her choice to be with him. She sometimes thought that she made the wrong decision while comparing Keegan and Roman, which sometimes led to regrets.

Months passed by, but he was still the same careless and inconsiderate person.

"I cannot deal with the way you are treating me. I am not the kind of person who deserves to be treated that way," she angrily cried to him.

"Okay, well, go find someone better who you deserve, and don't bother me."

With a response like that, she called it quits.

She chose to keep their breakup a secret for the time being, so she would be less embarrassed since that was what everyone had expected.

Despite that, she still talked to him and his family as usual. She would still go over by them and spend time with his mother.

It was mid-December, and it was time for Roman to graduate. He and Jayda remained friends and he wanted her to be there with him. He did fairly well and so she wanted to buy his graduation clothes.

It was difficult to get overtime work since everyone chose to work during the holidays, but shortly after, her friend offered to give her his overtime. He absented himself from work so she could fill in for him. Not very often you can find such kind people. But she was fortunate to have an encounter with Nate, who died a few months later.

Waking up at three every morning and reaching home after twelve at night was draining, but she kept it going.

Nevertheless, she was glad to be there during his achievement.

CHAPTER SIX

After months of ups and downs, breakups, and still sleeping together, they decided to reconcile their relationship. At midnight, New Year's 2011, he begged her for another chance, saying that he'd changed and he'd like to get more serious. Additionally, he kept saying that that girl was just a friend. Seeing it coming, she wasn't surprised. Her mind was saying no, but her heart was saying yes. It seemed as if her mind and heart had been programmed by him. Rosy did not want to move on to another man because she didn't want to be with multiple men.

After a long search, she finally found a job as a supervisor at the biggest and most popular boutique in town. She didn't quite like the job, but she took it anyway since it was approaching Roman birthday and she wanted to buy him a phone. By doing so, she went to purchase a phone, but the price was too high. Putting her pride aside again, she began to work overtime by cleaning up the store after work to earn extra cash. It was as if she never learned anything.

Right after collecting her salary, she quickly went to the store and bought the phone. She was so eager to give him that she skipped work that afternoon and went over by him.

It was approaching night, and the heavy wind blew her silky golden hair and covered her warm ivory face. He was there but his thoughts were on her short lace dress. As he drew closer to her, she could hear his heart beating. A million thoughts crossed her mind. It was dark; it was cold. She was alone with him. His big brown fingers brushed her hair across her seductive brown eyes. With his eyes closed, he passionately kissed her soft lips. He gently unzipped the back of her dress. He put his arms around her slim waist as he passionately grabbed her hair. Before they realized it, they were already in bed.

Two days after her birthday, he gifted her an exquisite necklace. It was the first time he ever gave her anything. She, however, didn't want to accept it because he had forgotten that her birthday had passed two days ago until Alice reminded him.

It is said that people don't change; they just hide who they are for a while. It seemed as though she was just his call girl who was a "babe" in bed and a stranger in public.

She loved him when her family and friends didn't. She stayed with him when he had nothing. And now that he was comfortable, he forsook her. That was major stress since she went through torture and torments, and she didn't leave but he did instead.

Hatred covered her heart that morning as she watched him texting another woman right before her eyes. She stood there, feeling betrayed as he hurled the phone towards the ground. She witnessed the phone that she bought him break into pieces the way he had her heart broken into pieces. She got so aggravated that she slapped him. Angrily, he yelled at her to get out of his sight.

She was so devastated that she used to cry herself to sleep at night, and woke up and cried again, but Marcus changed all that after time. Marcus was one of Jayda's best friends in school, whom she lost contact with and reunited with when she started her new job. Marcus was very educated and highly recognized in society. He would do whatever it took to make her feel better.

Hurt and distressed by the split, she needed someone to talk to, and since Britney wasn't around, she chose Marcus since she found comfort in him.

She allowed Roman to take advantage of her love for him. She became chronically unhappy, and as a result, she started to drink. When Marcus visited her at work that day, he was very disappointed in who she had become. After work, she started to go to the bar and tried to drown her problems away by getting drunk.

"I'm sorry, Rosy, but I don't like to see you like this, you're making things hard for me," Marcus said.

"What do you mean by that?" she questioned.

"I've been in love with you since high school, but I didn't have the courage to tell you. Now that you're not with that madman, I think that you should make a decision," he said.

"I'm also sorry, Marc, but I think you're just feeling sorry for me, besides, I just got out of a very toxic relationship and I'm not yet healed," said Rosia.

He did not allow her situation to get in the way by telling her how he felt about her. That was the last day they'd see each other, until four years later, when his father died.

She became sick due to depression, and as a result, she quit her job. It was too much for her to deal with at the moment. She invested a lot in the relationship, but it all led to disappointment.

She knew that it was about time that she needed to close that and accept that her love wasn't appreciated. Not because it was wrong, but because she gave it to someone who didn't deserve it. She went too deep in her emotions for him. She surrendered her power, trust, and everything to him, but that wasn't enough for him.

CHAPTER SEVEN

Finally, her dream of becoming a model came true. Most of the time she spent out of town and far from Roman. But at that time, he held onto her more than before because he thought that she would be a model and leave him for good.

He didn't want that because he had used it for her. She was doing well without him. She didn't even have the chance to miss him. She was regaining herself.

A few hours before the launching of Guyana's Next Top Model, Roman requested that she go over to help him with some chores. Since his family got back together and migrated to the USA, he lived by himself.

He had promised to represent her since every model was expected to have a date with him. Since modeling was her dream career, she wanted to take the first step with him. She didn't forget who he was to her when she had just an ordinary job.

Disappointed and with a heavy heart, she went to the launching herself since he had told her that he was too tired to go. He also added that he didn't want her to be a model.

She sadly said to him that he had no right to tell her what to do since they were not together anymore. She quickly grabbed her belongings and stormed out of the house. She wasn't too disappointed because she had seen it coming.

He wanted loyalty and consistency, but he couldn't give that to her; after all, she was his recycle bin. She oftentimes dried her tears and pulled herself together.

While he was rejecting her, other guys were trying to get her attention. The famous saying, "One man's garbage is another man's treasure." She was living proof that saying is true.

However, she was successful since she was getting recognition. That made her even bolder, but he kept degrading her. He discouraged her by telling her that she was not beautiful and that she couldn't be compared to the girls he was talking to. He was humiliating her, while others were praising her.

It was pathetic and woeful; it was a slap in the face witnessing how happy she was without him. He couldn't stand her happiness so he tried to manipulate her into getting back with him.

That day he was looking at some of the pictures she had taken and stumbled across the one that was taken with a local singer, a stunning young man whom she encountered at a fashion show. It was a friendly picture, but that was not how Roman saw it. He aggressively explained to her that he gave her a chance to be a model since she wanted to, but seeing her with another man hurt him since they were still friends. He somehow thought that he could still control her.

He was rude and detrimental, but she, on the other hand, tried to explain to him that the guy was just a friend. She also let him know that he had broken up with her in the first place, so why was he displaying such behavior?

"Rosy, I want what we had in the past," he said, but she said that she wanted better than what they had. With Roman trying to restore their broken relationship, she was trying not to get tangled in his web again. She had wanted that before she started modeling, but now that she was getting somewhere, she lost interest in him.

After all, she still cared about him. She requested that he give her some time to think about it. But that also came with a price since he wanted her to quit modeling.

While she was preparing for the semi-final, she explained to him that very soon the season would come to an end and that he should give her a chance. After considering all that she had gone through and that she had come this far, she promised him that she would drop out of the competition after that day. But he was so controlling and demanding that he wanted her to quit immediately.

She was so determined that she took the bus well-prepared for the next level. Distracted and worried, she went to the park and waited for the next bus.

He was confused as he answered his phone. It was Jayda asking him to pick her up at the park. To his astonishment, she didn't go to rehearsal. She is so that she would get disqualified from the competition.

The company called her the next day and asked her to go back; they explained to her that she had potential and they didn't want to lose such a talented and beautiful model.

She showed up the day after, but she had lost because she deliberately messed up her role. Choosing between love and a career wasn't simple for her since it was her dream to be a model, but also didn't want to lose him. She kept her relationship private, but she never kept him a secret.

She was happy that she was back with him, but she missed modeling. She also realized that dropping out wasn't a very wise thing to do since she had spent a lot of money.

Although the company called to give her another chance, she didn't take it.

After a week or two of a good relationship, she started to have problems with him again. Many nights, she stayed up late waiting for him to call and went to bed feeling unloved, betrayed, and taken for granted. He would, most of the time, make excuses that he worked late. But that was hardly an excuse.

That made her start to rethink and regret her choice. If only she could go back in time and change everything, she constantly thought to herself. She pretended to be happy but he never once noticed when she was sad. He never paid attention to her. He didn't even know that she wasn't happy with him, she was just happy that she had him. But he was still the one who could turn her day from gloomy to glory.

CHAPTER EIGHT

In the first part of 2013, he was a bit good to her. They had good and bad times as every couple should in a balanced and healthy relationship. She would normally go over by him.

Sometimes in the night, she would sneak out of the house to meet him. They did many fun things together. She treasured those precious moments.

She knew for a fact that he could change and become a better person if he wanted to. So she gave him a chance to discover himself.

She gave him time, but he was still irresponsible and immature. She felt as if she were the man in the relationship.

There were numerous times when she tried to hate him. Like those dark rainy nights when he made her walk by herself leaving her alone in the rain and drove away, thinking that it was okay for her to stand there all alone by herself on the road late at night waiting on a bus.

You never know how strong you are if you've never faced your fear. You never know how much someone means to you if you never have to fight for them. Moreover, you never know how much you can tolerate a narcissistic person if you have never experienced hard moments with them. But she overlooked all that.

She was convinced that he didn't love her, but she stayed with him because she was afraid to move on. She didn't want to lose him again. She was either too weak to leave or strong enough to stay.

Nevertheless, she was still good to him, and never told him how she felt about the situation because he never gave her a chance to explain herself. She felt trapped because whenever she talked about her feelings, it turned into an argument instead of a conversation.

They seemed to be getting along well now that she stopped complaining about how awful she treated her by flirting with other women in her presence. He would normally tell her that she was jealous whenever she tried to say how she felt.

In every relationship, a woman has the right to feel loved, wanted, and secure. Most men would compliment their woman, but not him. Instead, he gave other women the best compliments right in front of her. She generally felt like a whore in his bed. Even a whore was treated better than her.

There were, however, times when he was good to her. On his twenty-eighth birthday, she was almost shocked to death in front of him, but he saved her life. She was forever grateful to him. But apparently, he did it to torment her even more.

However, the suffering continued as she saw him paying attention to other women. She angrily looked at him, her eyes blazing with fierce indignation, and she said to him, "I never want to see you again, I have wasted so many years with you."

In response, he said, "Okay, I'm sorry that you felt that way, but she was just a friend, and I won't do anything to lose you again."

That day, she skipped her mother's birthday because he asked her to, and in return, he honored her by cheating on her again. The woman with whom he cheated couldn't even compare to half of what Jayda looked like. She wasn't even alluring, but just an average woman.

He, however, confirmed that he wanted a break from her, so she gave him the space he wanted. Some women wanted the diamond watch, while some valued the time, but even his time she had enough of. Now that he extirpated her, he left her.

She had no one to talk to since Alice got married and migrated to another country, so she turned to God.

This time, she did not chase after him; she fasted without food and water for six months and cried out to God to heal her heart and get over him. She asked God that if he is not for her, then let him go and never return. But instead, something else happened. She was no longer a slave to her emotions. While he was out there having fun with another, she was trying to heal from the damage he caused.

He did not return immediately, but months later, he came as if nothing happened. After she explained to him that she didn't deserve him but someone better, he dared to tell her that she couldn't have another man because he was all that she could ever have while adding that she belonged to only him.

She found a job and he went on a vacation with his family. That was somehow the best time for her after a long time. She made new friends; she even reconnected with old ones. She was having the time of her life. She somewhat saw the bright side of life. She then realized that love wasn't everything. As a result, she paid more attention to herself, her job, and other loved ones.

CHAPTER NINE

She was busy cleaning up her desk at work when her eyes caught his captivating eyes. She smiled at him with a newly established boldness that he found alluring. It was an instant attraction. Their eyes saw each other, but their souls felt each other. She felt a passionate spark immediately as he said, "Hi" to her. It was someone she had known for a long time. He also knew who she was. They knew each other. He constantly occupied her mind.

Days and weeks passed, but she couldn't stop thinking about him. But he was just part of her fantasy. They didn't see each other often; it was until Roman had gone on his vacation.

When he returned home, he insisted that she move in with him but she had just started her new job as a sales representative. The only sales representative for that branch. She somehow thought that that would create conflicts with her job.

Without thinking about it, she moved in with her verbally abusive boyfriend, but it wasn't what she had expected.

He was very affectionate towards her. He treated her like a delicate flower that never had been plucked. While she was at work, he would help out at home. Sometimes he cooked dinner, or at times, took her out. It was the sort of relationship she had dreamed of. He would take her to work and pick her up after work. She was positively ecstatic. Even though he sometimes left her alone at night to hang out with his friends, she overlooked most of his flaws. Instead, she started to respect him once again. But she wasn't naive; she knew that he had something up his sleeve. It all seemed too good to be true.

But as they say, "After laugh is cry." She became his servant while he was out there enjoying himself, she had to do everything. The sad thing was that she couldn't go to sleep if he were not home. If she ever did, he would wake her up and violently swear at her.

If she treated him the way he treated her, he would leave. She, however, coped with all that until late one Wednesday night at 10:00, his phone rang. She answered and it was a woman; she rudely told her not to call back. She immediately packed her belongings and left the house. He was there trying to convince her not to.

The next morning, he was there at her workplace. He apologized, saying that he was very sorry, and that he wanted to marry her. But then she remembered how he threw her out of the house before, in the middle of the night. She was there all by herself. She knew that she would be trapped at home. Her work was her freedom and privilege. She knew her worth and her value. She did not go back with him.

It had somehow come as a blessing since his parents came back for a short vacation. This somewhat had brought them back close together since his parents were there for her. But they insisted that she quit her job, which she didn't hesitate to do. They gave themselves another chance as usual.

However, their fight to survive the relationship was far from easy. Roman and Rosia bravely endured the period of financial turmoil together with love. He tried to make her happy. Their relationship somewhat became what she deserved. They became each other's happiness. No one is perfect; we all have flaws, but sometimes we have to overlook them in others because they overlook ours.

She hugged him tightly without a drop of tears and with a heart full of emotions, as she watched him walk away. They bid each other "Adieu." She stood there in the rain as she watched the plane until it vanished into the heavy clouds.

Their live-in relationship came to an end, since it was time he had to reside in the United States of America.

Now the distance became their new test of love. Every day is a new hope. "I'll wait for you for however long it takes," she said to herself.

But would she?

CHAPTER TEN

It is said, "Out of sight, out of mind."

It'd been six months since Roman had gone; there came the guy who captivated her with his mysterious smile. She admired his smile for a while. He melted her heart with his cruel gaze. The way he always looked at her was mesmerizing. Rosia and Rogan became close as they were involved in each other's lives. However, he was just a friend who fulfilled her sexual desires.

She always knew that he was also attracted to her, which he confirmed that night when he mysteriously opened up to her. She understood him; he understood her.

"Don't come into my dreams without knocking," she said to him, as she ended their three-hour call that night. She was convinced that she was desperate for his love, and he was for hers.

Their first meeting was a night to remember. She saw the desire in his honey brown eyes for her. As he held her in his arms, she passionately kissed him. As sparks increased, he had her on her knees, her hair wrapped around his fist as they made deep eye contact. Afterwards, he aggressively grabbed her neck from behind. He wrapped his huge hands around her throat while his tongue slid into her mouth. It amped up her raging desires, as he thrusted deep inside her. "It feels good, doesn't it, babe?" he growled.

"It does, I want more of you," she whispered. His body entwined with hers. On a cold, rainy night, they were on a heated fire that could only be extinguished by pleasure as they made love. His soul made love to hers before their bodies met.

He was her motivation. He was there for her when she took her first step to becoming a fashion designer. He became her strength and courage. He helped her conquer her fear. He made her feel important and loved. It felt like they were in different bodies, but their hearts are always synchronized.

They were grateful for each other's company.

She realized that they were meeting too often and decided to avoid him. But he did not allow her to forget him since he constantly reminded her of what they had. But she tried to run away from the memories. Many times, she tried to disregard her feelings, doubting herself that she didn't want him.

She begins to miss him, not only her body, but her soul desires him. It was difficult for her to stay away from him now. After all, she ended up giving herself to him.

They were never seen together in public but behind closed doors. He was her desire, her passion. They were just two friends making memories too good to tell. Taking chances of making love in a world of ecstasy. Every self-control was lost that night. He is impulsive and passionate.

"Call my name," he demanded, as he planted a soft kiss on her thigh.

Her damp underwear is just an inch away from his mouth. It was nights of endless pleasures. As they showered together, he helped wash away her fears. That night, she didn't just look into his eyes but his soul as well. She wanted him more that night, more than before, and she became his passion.

Since the dawn of civilization, women have allowed themselves to be used by men as an instrument of pleasure and lust, but it was different with Rogan and Rosia because they both used each other for pleasure at some point in time.

They involuntarily became serious with their sexual relationship. They respect each other more, and they become stronger together. He became her weakness, and she became his strength. They both shared the same energy and that kept them stronger together. She changed his life, and he was more ebullient now because of her. Their relationship had no pressure as they gave each other space, but even with freedom, they were glued to each other. He was ice, cold, and heartless, and she was the fire that melted his cold heart.

CHAPTER ELEVEN

"It's a year now since we're dating, and I think we should do something special tomorrow," Rogan suggested. He had wanted everyone to know about their secret affair.

"Today is the day; it's about time," she thought to herself.

"Rogan, I've been waiting for this day more than you do."

That afternoon, she wore that red dress for the first time. She matched it with a classy pair of heels. She looked so ravishing that he stood up upon her arrival. He gazed at her with sincerity in his eyes. His gaze was the promise of protection and more. He admired her for a while, thinking to himself, "How beautiful she is."

He won't let anything get in the way of expressing his true feelings for her. He enthusiastically thought to himself that with Roman out of the picture, no one was there to come in between them like he did while they dated.

But it was not like that; Rosia and Roman were still very much in love with each other. Rogan was one of Roman's friends. He always had his eyes on her for quite a long time, so he couldn't wait to get his hands on her. Rosia, being a smart girl, knew his weakness and fiddled him like a pack of cards.

"It's over now, I cannot do this anymore," she bravely looked into his eyes with hatred and love at the same time.

"I've had my revenge, and I don't need you anymore."

As she spoke, she looked away to avoid eye contact with him.

"What are you saying, what revenge?" He looked at her with a puzzled mind.

After explaining to him the reason for vengeance, he was emotionally traumatized to know that the girl he left standing there with the crowd waiting for him to show up was her close friend, Zoey.

Zoey was eager as she was getting dressed for her twenty-seventh birthday party. It was an auspicious day for her. She was excessively ecstatic as she put on her seafoam green dress. Her face glows while smiling at her mother. It was almost midnight and there was no sign of him, not even a phone call. Everyone was getting worried since they were supposed to get engaged that night.

Zoey was there, crying her eyes out when everyone advised her to change her clothes and they encouraged her not to wait any longer.

Without an explanation, he apologized to her the next day. It was the end of their relationship. Zoey was left dejected and thought of suicide.

Rosia planned to make him fall in love with her and leave him like he left her friend. On the other hand, she had satisfaction since she took revenge on Roman as well for all the times he cheated on her.

She left him standing there as she walked away, thinking whether or not she should seek his forgiveness. He was her sweet misfortune.

A month later, she wondered if she should call or let him go.

"Roman, we should start over, and I promise to be honest this time," Rosia said.

"I can't blame you if you choose not to be with me after everything I did to you. It's okay, Rose, I deserved it, but I want you, I want us," he replied.

As they were about to kiss, she was awakened by the ringing of her phone. It was Roman; he called to inform her that he would be there in two days.

CHAPTER TWELVE

She sat in front of her mirror doing her makeup; her hair was in gorgeous curls. She felt like a princess when her mother placed a sparkly tiara on her head, as the white veil hid her beautiful face and so did her feelings for Rogan. She closed her bedroom door and grabbed her phone as she looked back at his picture one more time. "If only he knew that I'd loved him too."

She never thought that he would take up such a huge space in her heart. Yet still, she was remorseful for what she had done to him and Roman.

Her heart was at peace as she placed the ring on his finger. He looked even more handsome than ever. He was a better person now. Looking at him, she saw her future in his eyes. As they took their vows, she knew that next to him was where she belonged.

She was overwhelmed but still worried if she would ever be happy being his wife. The struggles he put her through the years had made her paranoid. She wondered if she would survive a marriage with him for a lifetime.

A few months after they were married, he still couldn't get her out of his mind, but Rosia let it be because she understood the feelings of loving someone from afar. After all, she had feelings for Rogan but couldn't be with him.

It wasn't supposed to happen like that. It was supposed to be the beginning of a beautiful marriage. But just as she suspected he was cheating on her with Ursula, the same woman whom he called decent. She had always been the third person in Rosia and Roman's relationship.

But being in two different countries, why did he still feel the need to talk to her instead of his wife? A woman who was married and had kids. However, both women lived in Guyana. Being in a long-distance relationship was both good and bad for Rosia.

She then regretted dumping Rogan while he was still trying to win her back. Her husband pushed her to another man daily by treating her cruelly. Because of him, she gave up on herself, but Rogan reminded her of how important she was. What Roman didn't show her, Rogan did. But she chose not to go back to him, even though she had wanted to. She wanted to be the better one in their marriage. She didn't give up on her husband, the same man she called her life partner.

The most insidious thing about his cheating was that she suffered infidelity, which made it impossible to trust him again. She made it difficult for Ursula since her husband intervened, so trying to break Rosia and Roman's marriage was a failed plan for her.

She was trying to show the world how decent and trustworthy she is, but behind her husband's back, she was an insidious snake. She failed as a wife, and Roman failed as a husband. For Rosia, he was not husband material. He was destroying his marriage with his own hands. What he did to her never healed, and thus, she lived with the hurt and betrayal every day. She finally realized that she had done enough for their relationship. Her love for him was slowly dying.

CHAPTER THIRTEEN

"I'm so glad that I will see you again. I miss you a lot, babe, I know you miss me too. Please tell me you do," he said to her.

"Well of course I do, I miss you like crazy," she replied with a warm smile. He gently rubbed his hands on her face as she shivered at his penetrating gaze. They met again in such a lonely state. He picked her up from class that cloudy evening. That was the first day they saw each other after nine months. She wasn't expecting him to be in the city that day, but he knew where she was.

"Rogan, keep your eyes on the road, and not on me," she said.

"It's okay, love. I know what I'm doing, your beauty is distracting me," he said, smiling at her.

Like hot embers, her desires started to emerge as he slowly rubbed his hands on her thighs. He couldn't help but stop the car and kiss her. He gently brushed her hair aside and put his hands around her neck. She swiftly got in his shirt and grabbed his muscles. She then passionately unzipped his pants. No one could see because the windows were foggy since it rained. The drops mixed with the car lights seemed like golden rain.

"Baby, I want you, every part of you, to quench my thirst with your love. You're still mine, and you know it. You are mine forever," he whispered in her ear. "You're already wet for me, baby."

"And I want you inside me, I want to feel your heartbeat through my breast," she said.

Sparks started to flow as he slightly licked her neck.

Their emotions reconnected with each other.

That moment belonged to them. They lived in the moment. Their energy matched; they were compatible without trying.

She looked at him with every stroke as he held her tight in his arms.

He whispered, "You make me happy. You own me, every inch of me belongs to you, baby. I love you with every fiber of my being."

The temptations send a shiver down her spine. She's his captive, and she can't stop wanting him. They couldn't get any closer than they were to each other that night. Rogan and Rosia's love affair reignited.

She couldn't think of anything else because of how ecstatic she was about him. She knew that it would be hard to leave this time since he was always there in her lonely times.

They united in such a way like two bodies but one soul.

She knew that their relationship wouldn't last forever, but his love was a poisonous addiction to her. He was her inspiration, the one person who never underestimated her.

They knew that they wouldn't be together forever, so they spent a lot of time together. Time was everything for them.

They were just so kind to each other. It was like it was too good to be true. She sometimes slept over by him. They did things that a real couple did. They started to spend more time together. Their connections were real. They were head over heels in love with each other, so much so that they completed each other. Rosia finally found someone to be happy with.

They made precious memories together. Rogan adored her so much that sometimes she questioned herself if she deserved his love. They even got matching tattoos with each other's initials. They completely consumed each other.

"I can't wait to see you tonight, my love, I'm so excited."

"This is going to be the best sleepover," he said to her with excitement. His eyes sparkled with anticipation.

"I love you, baby," he said.

"I love you too," she replied as she ended their video call.

Tangling his fingers in her hair, he captured her mouth with his. He looks into her eyes with his hands buried in her hair. "Just a reminder that you belong to me. I own you, you're mine."

"You're my dearest property. You're not gonna leave me, you are going to endure my existence for as long as we live. You are infinitely mine."

"You are my golden rose forever," Rogan growled possessively. He kissed her with passion.

"You taste so good," he said with a smirk.

His hands are tight on her wrist while his tongue goes deep inside her. He filled her up so deep that she couldn't help but scream his name out loud.

"That's right, babe, call my name when I'm devouring you. Now tell me that you're mine," he commanded.

"I'm all yours, baby," she said softly.

"Now open up for me like a good girl, I'm not finished with you as yet." He murmured looking at her with ardent passion.

With every mess that he made of her, he cleaned it up with his tongue.

After helping her get into his shirt, he gently kissed her forehead.

"Babe, I know I'm not everything you need, but I will never stop trying. I know you're married, but babe, I do not want to separate from you, ever again. I'm not trying to break your marriage, but also don't break me, please, babe. It took forever to find you and it would take an eternity to let you go. You're the puzzle to my heart. You're my once-in-a-life-time," he confessed.

"Rogan, you are very important to me, and I don't want to even imagine what my life would be like without you. I love, and I love us. I absolutely love what we have. I promise to be with you for as long as you want me to. But I promise to love you forever. I love you infinitely," Rosia replied.

"What do you mean, for as long as I want you to be?" I want you to be with me forever, babe," Rogan replied.

"Rose, I'm in love with you and you know that. I have deep feelings for you. You are made for me. I don't ever want to lose you again."

"Do you hear me?"

"You complete me. I can't live without you anymore. You will never, ever be unloved by me," he said.

As he went down on his knees, he had in his hands a gold box. In it was a red rose.

"A rose for a rose," he said.

"Rose, I promise to love, protect, and cherish you forever. I am so lucky and blessed to have you in my life."

"I love you infinitely, baby, and I will do anything to make you happy. And this is a promise from me to you," he said.

Shortly after they exchanged rings. Those rings were the rings of promise to continue love, care, and be with each other. That day marks three years of their relationship.

"Rogan, all I can say is, 'thank you, my love.' I'm happy being with you. I love you for who you are. Thank you for everything. You are my golden love," she replied while she gently kissed his forehead.

She knew that being with him is not the right thing to do, but it was not a crime either. And so they were both happy in each other's company.

That morning, they woke early. She was apprehensive, and so was he. They made breakfast together. It was something Rosia had always dreamed of. They enjoyed every moment together. It was time for her to leave. Tears fell from her eyes as he gently kissed her and said, "Bye bye, for now my love."

"I'll see you next two weeks, and remember I love you. I will wait for you."

"I love you and I will miss you. I can't wait to see you again," she replied.

He looked at her as she got out of the car and instantly got wet in the rain. She looked back at him one last time, blowing him a kiss before she entered her house.

CHAPTER FOURTEEN

She's with him but all she could think of was Rogan. She was supposed to be happy to see her husband, but she was wistful for a moment until Roman asked if she was okay. She had to pretend that she was happy. She was somewhat wondering if Rogan would change his mind about her. After all, she was married but he wasn't. Nevertheless, she had some faith. She was, however, trying to get him out of her mind and thoughts.

He was completely submerged in her thoughts. She was even more convinced that she was indeed in love with Rogan.

However, she tried to adjust and let her husband in, but Roman had noticed the changes in her. She tried to convince him that everything was okay and that it was just her being a bit stressed from all the outings. But her heart, she was crying out loud. Her eyes were craving to see Rogan whenever they went out.

It was late Thursday night and Roman had gone out with his friends. It was approaching 2:00 am and he was still not home as yet. She was getting worried since he didn't take his phone with him. She then realized that he hadn't changed.

After reaching home at four in the morning, all he said to her was that he hung out with Rogan a bit. She did not know what happened that night but Roman seemed angrier and more caring at the same time. That created more emotional space between him and his wife. However, they made use of the little time they had together.

CHAPTER FIFTEEN

"So are you gonna tell him about the baby?" Lucy asked.

"Umm, I don't know, should I?" Rosai asked.

"I think you should, after all, he's the father, and now that Roman is not here you have the perfect opportunity," Lucy suggested.

"You know what, Lucy?" I don't think that I should, since we haven't spoken since Roman came. We were supposed to meet after two weeks, but he still hasn't returned my call and it has been weeks now," Rosia replied with settled tears in her eyes.

Rogan and Rosia's love was unknown to everyone, but she was so depressed that she decided to open up to her friend Lucy.

Lucy and Rosia had known each other ever since she had started to date Roman. They weren't that close until Roman migrated. Lucy was always there for her, as she was for Lucy. They started to spend more time together and so they had earned each other's trust. Now that Lucy knew everything about Rogan and Rosia, their friendship became more genuine.

Lucy did everything in her power to help Rosia to get over Rogan, but nothing helped. Until one day, she decided to pray about it. But all she ever asked God for was to protect him and be with him wherever he was. She kept praying for him to be happy wherever he was. She tried to get over him, but she couldn't. She then realized that as much as she wanted him to show up, she also wanted him to be happy, with or without her.

Her mind keeps replaying what her heart cannot delete. Her heart cried continuously for him. She knew that her feelings for him would never change, but she also felt that deep down in his heart, there were feelings for her as well. She lives with the hopes that within time he will show up, and she will get to see him again even if it is just a glimpse.

She couldn't forget his precious smile and his fragrance, or how he had cared for her. But most of all she couldn't forget how she felt when she was with him. Their connection was rare. He was not with her, yet still, she could feel his presence. She could hear his voice in her head telling her how much he loved her. Each memory was filled with his story. But she was thankful and considered herself blessed to have experienced such closeness with him. It's like they were made for each other but still got separated. And so she lived each day wondering what went wrong. She tried to convince herself that he didn't love her and that she needed to get over him.

But was it working?

CHAPTER SIXTEEN

Seeing him after some time, life had brought books of past days. What the heart hides, the eyes reveal. She admired him for a few minutes, thinking of how handsome he was. Her eyes got wet when she looked at him, remembering that he was once part of her life. Trying to control her emotions, she smiled at him. It's hard not to show until it all crumbled and her tears shamefully fell. In her heart, there were burning lamps of desires for him. She could still see the love for her in his eyes. He also had on the ring she gave him. She still questioned herself as to why she had to see such dark days.

But feelings that came back were feelings that never left.

"I will love you forever, I care about you more than you know. I promised to protect you at whatever cost. Even if it's letting you go," he said softly with settled tears in his eyes.

"Why did you do this to me? I waited for you all day hoping that you would show up. I don't like you anymore. You broke every one of your promises. You promised to be with me forever, that you will never stop trying. So what happens now? Why aren't we together?" She aggressively shouted at him.

"And I did keep my promises, Rose. Right now, I am living up to the promises that I made to you, and not everything you have to know. Remember, you are and always be my 'GOLDEN LOVE,'" he said while wiping her tears away.

Her name was announced, and it was time for her to receive her award as best fashion designer of the year. She looked back for him, but he was nowhere to be found. She loved him with every beat of her heart. All she left with was his memories; she missed him every day but mostly when it rained She could not unlove him; he was tangled in her soul.

Neither were they friends, nor were they enemies. They were just two strangers with precious memories. Rogan was Rosia's soulmate, but Roman was her life partner. Rosia and Rogan's love did not reach its destination, or maybe that was its destination. He was her once upon a time but not her happy ending. However, she still felt in her heart that they were meant to be.

THE END

www.ingramcontent.com/pod-product-compliance
Lightning Source LLC
Chambersburg PA
CBHW052227150726
48002CB00003B/1309